CONTENTS

The world of science ⟶ **4**

Light ⟶ **6**

Sound ⟶ **8**

Q Go quiz yourself! ⟶ **10**

Energy ⟶ **12**

Electricity ⟶ **14**

Q Go quiz yourself! ⟶ **16**

Forces ⟶ **18**

Magnets ⟶ **20**

Q Go quiz yourself! ⟶ **22**

Materials ⟶ **24**

Solids, liquids and gases ⟶ **26**

Q Go quiz yourself! ⟶ **28**

Living things ⟶ **30**

Plants ⟶ **32**

Q Go quiz yourself! ⟶ **34**

Ancient science ⟶ **36**

Amazing inventions ⟶ **38**

Q Go quiz yourself! ⟶ **40**

The future of science ⟶ **42**

Answers ⟶ **44**

Glossary ⟶ **46**

Further information ⟶ **47**

Index ⟶ **48**

HOW TO USE THIS BOOK

This book is packed full of amazing facts and statistics. When you've finished reading a section, test yourself with questions on the following page. Check your answers on pages 44–45 and see if you're a quizmaster or if you need to quiz it again! When you've finished, test your friends and family to find out who's the ultimate quiz champion!

THE WORLD OF SCIENCE

Science helps us to understand the natural world and the way it works. Scientists are constantly discovering incredible facts that make us see the world around us in a whole new light.

TYPES OF SCIENCE

We often divide science into three main categories:

Biology – the science of life and living things

Chemistry – the science of elements and compounds

Physics – the science of the way the physical world works

MANY DIFFERENT TOPICS ARE STUDIED IN EACH AREA OF SCIENCE

Biology

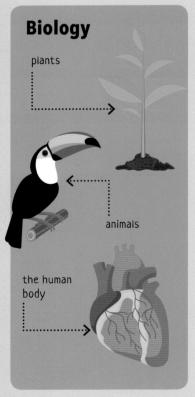

plants

animals

the human body

Chemistry

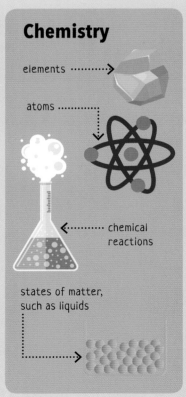

elements ·······>

atoms ·······

chemical reactions

states of matter, such as liquids

Physics

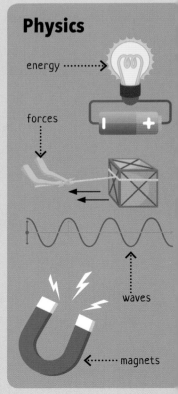

energy ·······>

forces

waves

magnets

Water can exist as a solid, liquid and gas
at the same time!
This can only happen in certain conditions at 0.01 °C.

Find out more about solids, liquids and gases on pages 26–27.

There is no sound in space!
This is because there are very few particles in space to vibrate, so sound waves can't travel.

Find out more about sound waves on pages 8–9.

Studying science has helped us to uncover some amazing facts.

There is enough electricity in the human brain when awake to power a
small lightbulb!

Find out more about electricity on pages 14–15.

Pancakes are usually round because of
GRAVITY!
The force of gravity pulls on the pancake batter evenly, forming it into a circle.

Find out more about forces on pages 18–19.

Some species of bamboo can grow up to a
metre in one day!

Find out more about plants on pages 32–33.

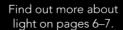

SCORPIONS GLOW
in the light of a full moon!

Find out more about light on pages 6–7.

LIGHT

Light allows us to see objects. It reflects off objects and into our eyes.

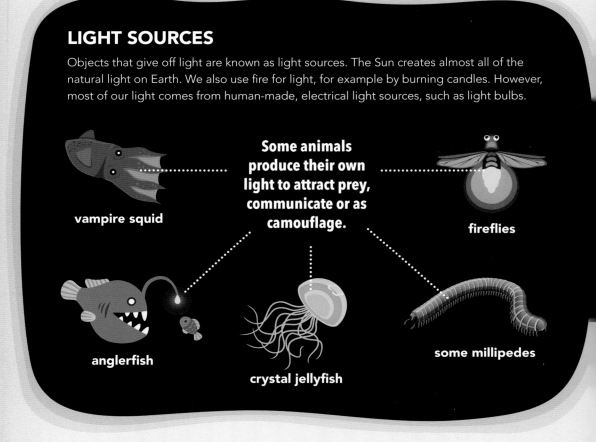

LIGHT SOURCES

Objects that give off light are known as light sources. The Sun creates almost all of the natural light on Earth. We also use fire for light, for example by burning candles. However, most of our light comes from human-made, electrical light sources, such as light bulbs.

Some animals produce their own light to attract prey, communicate or as camouflage.

vampire squid

fireflies

anglerfish

crystal jellyfish

some millipedes

MATERIALS

Light can only pass through some materials. Transparent materials, such as glass, let light through. Translucent materials, such as coloured plastic, let some light through. Opaque materials, such as wood, don't let any light through.

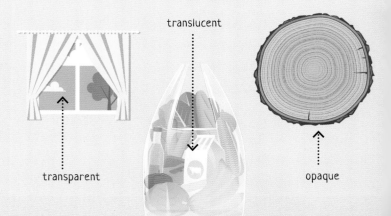

translucent

transparent

opaque

SHADOWS

When light is blocked by a translucent or opaque object, it creates a dark shadow behind the object. The size and shape of the shadow depend on the size and position of the light source.

BENDING LIGHT

Usually light travels in straight lines, known as rays. However, rays of light can bend when they travel from one material to another. This is because they move more quickly through one material than another. This is called refraction.

The bottom of the pencil appears to be in the wrong place. This is because the light bends as it moves between the air and the water in the glass.

SEEING COLOUR

Light is a mixture of all colours. We see objects as coloured because of the way the surface of the object reflects or absorbs the colours in light. If an object reflects all the colours of light, we see it as white. Some objects reflect just one colour and absorb the rest. We see these objects as the reflected colour, for example red. If an object absorbs all of the colours, we see it as black.

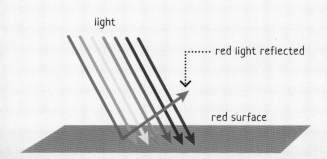

light

red light reflected

red surface

BIG, BLUE SKY

Air is transparent, but we see the sky as blue. This is because sunlight reflects off tiny particles in the air and gets scattered across the sky. Blue light is scattered more than other colours, giving the sky its blue colour.

SOUND

Sound is created when objects vibrate, sending sound waves through the air. These waves enter the ear, where they are understood as sounds.

PITCH

Pitch is how high or low a sound is. The speed of the vibrations determines the pitch of a sound. Fast vibrations make high-pitched sounds, while slow vibrations make low-pitched sounds. Animals, such as dogs, have a wider range of hearing than humans and can hear sounds that we can't.

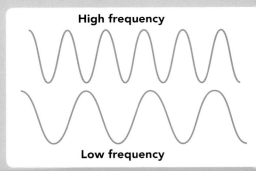

High frequency

Low frequency

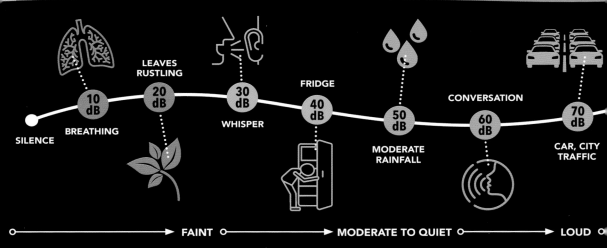

LEAVES RUSTLING

10 dB

20 dB

30 dB

FRIDGE

40 dB

50 dB

CONVERSATION

60 dB

70 dB

SILENCE

BREATHING

WHISPER

MODERATE RAINFALL

CAR, CITY TRAFFIC

FAINT ○━━━━▶ MODERATE TO QUIET ○━━━━▶ LOUD ○

VOLUME

Volume is how loud something is. It is measured in decibels (dB). The taller a sound wave, the louder the noise. Loud sounds can damage the ear, so it's best to avoid them or wear ear protection in noisy situations, such as loud concerts or while using noisy machinery.

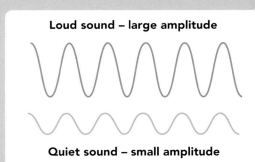

Loud sound – large amplitude

Quiet sound – small amplitude

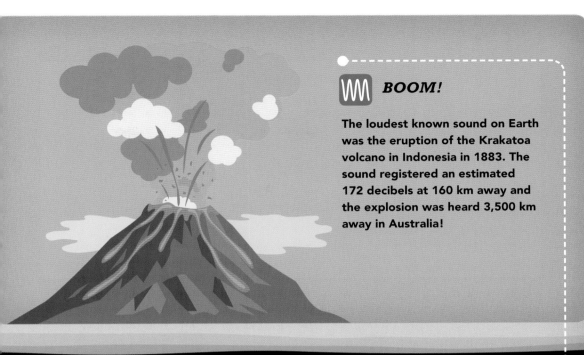

The loudest known sound on Earth was the eruption of the Krakatoa volcano in Indonesia in 1883. The sound registered an estimated 172 decibels at 160 km away and the explosion was heard 3,500 km away in Australia!

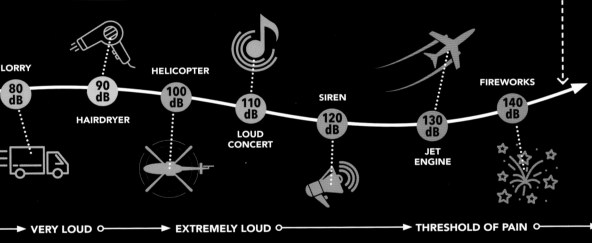

LORRY
80 dB

90 dB
HAIRDRYER

HELICOPTER
100 dB

110 dB
LOUD CONCERT

SIREN
120 dB

130 dB
JET ENGINE

FIREWORKS
140 dB

→ VERY LOUD ○ → EXTREMELY LOUD ○ → THRESHOLD OF PAIN ○

ECHOES

An echo is a repeated sound. Echoes are created when sound waves bounce off some objects and are reflected back to you so that you hear them again. Only hard objects create echoes, which is why they are commonly heard in tunnels or caves with hard walls. Soft objects absorb sound waves, so no echoes are heard.

Ships use echoes to find items underwater, such as fish. This system is called sonar. Ships send out sound waves that bounce off underwater objects. They use the reflected sound waves to know where the objects are.

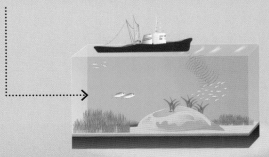

1 What is studied in biology?

2 Which area of science studies magnets and energy?

3 Why are pancakes usually round?

4 Which animal glows in the light of a full moon?

5 What is a light source?

6 Name an animal that produces its own light.

7 Which word describes a material that doesn't let any light through?

8 When are shadows formed?

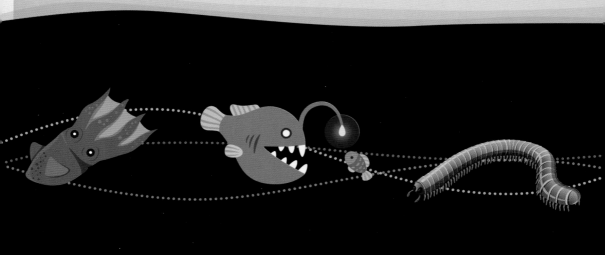

---> **9** If an object absorbs all colours of light, what colour do we see it as?

10 Why does the sky look blue?

11 If sound waves vibrate slowly, what pitch is the sound?

12 Who has better hearing – humans or dogs?

13 Which unit do we use to measure volume?

14 How many decibels is the sound of an average conversation?

15 What is the loudest known sound on Earth?

16 Why are echoes often heard in tunnels?

17 What is sonar?

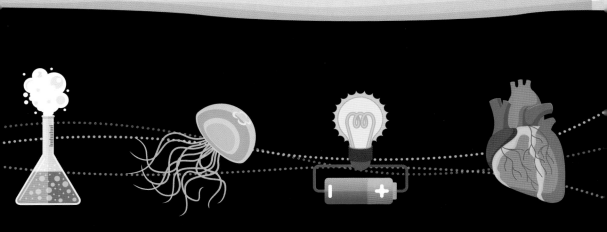

ENERGY

Energy makes things work. Every action requires energy, from moving and breathing to powering vehicles and machines.

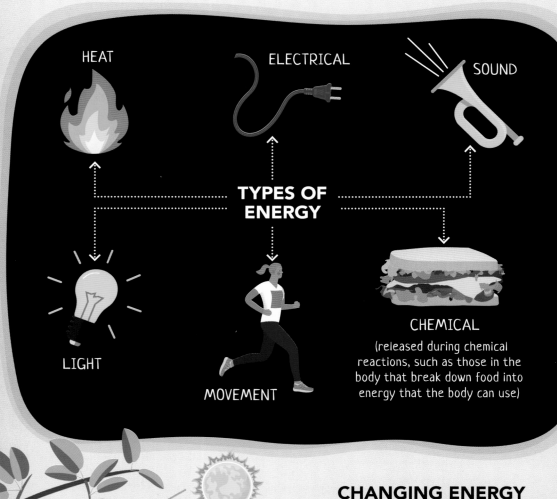

TYPES OF ENERGY

HEAT

ELECTRICAL

SOUND

LIGHT

MOVEMENT

CHEMICAL
(released during chemical reactions, such as those in the body that break down food into energy that the body can use)

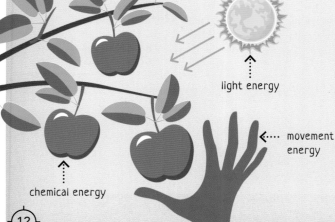

light energy

movement energy

chemical energy

CHANGING ENERGY

Energy can be changed from one form to another. For example, electrical energy is turned into heat energy in a microwave or a toaster. Our bodies convert chemical energy from food into movement and heat to keep us warm. Plants turn light energy from the Sun into chemical energy (food).

coal-fired power plant

GENERATING ELECTRICITY

There are several different ways of converting energy into electricity.

wind turbines

In fossil fuel power plants, chemical energy from fossil fuels is turned into heat energy when the fuels are burned. The heat energy is used to boil water, which creates steam. The steam spins a turbine (movement energy), which powers a generator that creates electricity.

In hydroelectric dams and wind turbines, movement energy from flowing water or wind spins a turbine, which powers a generator that creates electricity.

ENVIRONMENTAL PROBLEMS

Some energy sources create environmental problems. Burning fossil fuels creates air pollution and releases greenhouse gases, such as carbon dioxide. Greenhouse gases gather in the atmosphere and trap heat from the Sun close to Earth's surface. This increases the temperature on Earth (global warming) which disrupts natural habitats and changes weather patterns. Air pollution also leads to health problems, such as asthma and certain types of cancer.

GLOBAL WARMING

The average world temperature has increased by 0.8 °C since 1880 because of global warming.

ELECTRICITY

Electricity is a type of energy. There are two types of electricity – current and static.

CURRENT ELECTRICITY

This type of electricity is found in circuits in buildings. It is used to power lights and appliances. Batteries also produce current electricity. A chemical reaction inside the battery generates the electricity.

CIRCUITS

A circuit is a path that electricity travels around, made up of wires and a source of electricity, such as a battery. Circuits can also contain other components, such as light bulbs, motors and buzzers. Switches are used to control circuits. A circuit has to be complete for electricity to flow around it. When a switch is open, it stops the flow of electricity around the circuit. When a switch is closed, the circuit is complete and electricity flows around the circuit.

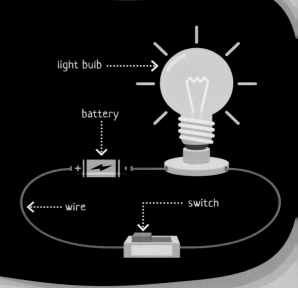

light bulb

battery

wire

switch

CONDUCTORS AND INSULATORS

Electricity moves differently through different materials. Conductors are materials that electricity passes through easily. Electricity does not pass through materials that are insulators. We use insulators to keep electricity safe. For example, plastic insulation on the outside of electrical wires stops the electricity from escaping.

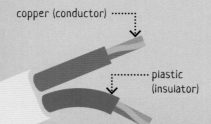

copper (conductor)

plastic (insulator)

CONDUCTORS	INSULATORS
copper	plastic
iron	wood
steel	glass
water	rubber

STATIC ELECTRICITY

When two insulators rub together, tiny electrically-charged particles called electrons jump from one material to the other. This build-up of electrons creates static electricity.

If you run a comb through your hair, it builds up a static charge and so the comb will be able to attract and pick up tiny bits of paper.

NATURAL ELECTRICITY

Electricity exists in nature. Lightning is static electricity that builds up in clouds. It is released down to the ground during storms. Animals, including humans, also generate electricity inside their bodies. A very small amount of electricity is used to send messages to and from the brain and make the heart beat. Some animals generate large amounts of electricity and use it to hunt and kill prey.

NATURAL ELECTRICITY

★ The longest ever lightning bolt measured the distance from London, UK, to Brussels, Belgium.

★ The longest ever duration of a lightning bolt was 7.74 seconds. The average duration of a lightning bolt is 0.2 seconds.

★ Lightning is five times hotter than the surface of the Sun.

★ Sharks have special electricity sensors on their skin. They use the sensors to sense the electrical signals in nearby prey.

★ Electric eels sent out huge jolts of electricity to kill their prey.

GO QUIZ YOURSELF!

18 Name two types of energy.

19 What type of energy is food?

20 Describe the energy conversion that happens in a microwave.

21 Which two types of energy do our bodies create from chemical energy?

22 How is electricity generated in a hydroelectric dam?

23 What is a greenhouse gas?

24 Name a health problem caused by air pollution.

25 How much has the average world temperature increased since 1880?

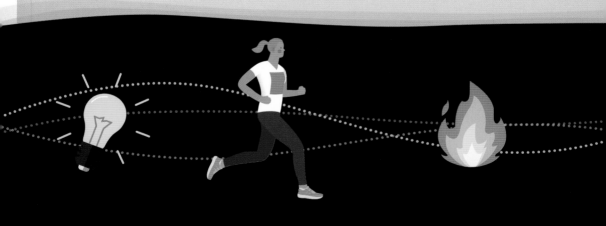

----→ **26** What are the two types of electricity?

27 Give an example of a component found in a circuit.

28 What happens to a circuit if its switch is open?

29 Name two materials that are electrical insulators.

30 What type of electricity is lightning?

31 How long did the longest ever lightning bolt last?

32 Which is hotter – lightning or the surface of the Sun?

33 Name one way in which electricity is used in the bodies of most animals and humans.

34 Which animal uses electricity to kill their prey?

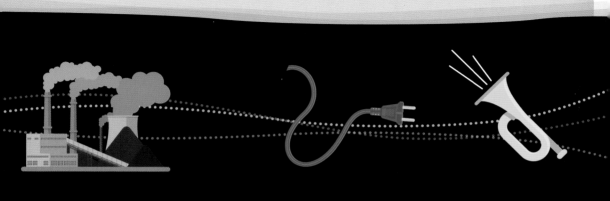

FORCES

Forces are pushes or pulls. They can make things move, change speed, change shape and change direction.

FORCES AND OBJECTS

The stronger a force, the greater an effect it will have on an object. Some objects need to touch for a force to have an effect, such as when a foot kicks a ball. Other forces, such as gravity, can affect objects without touching them.

FRICTION

Friction is the force that acts on an object when it moves against another object. It acts in the opposite direction to the movement of the object, which can make it hard for the object to move. Smooth surfaces have very little friction, while rough surfaces have more. Friction can be useful – it stops our feet from slipping on the ground.

GRAVITY

Gravity is a force that pulls objects towards each other. All objects have gravity, but heavier objects have more gravity than lighter ones. The heaviest object near to us is Earth. Its gravity pulls everything around us down to its surface. This is why objects fall to the ground if they are dropped.

There is very little friction on smooth ice and snow, which is why skis glide easily across them.

RESISTANCE

When an object moves through air or water, it experiences resistance created by friction. This resistance slows the object down and makes it have to push harder to move through the air or water. The faster an object travels, the more resistance it experiences. Streamlined (with a smooth shape) objects experience less resistance and can move more quickly through air or water.

BALANCING FORCES

If two forces of the same size act on an object in opposite directions, nothing will happen to the object. It will stay still or keep moving at the same speed. This is because the forces are balanced.

However, if one force is greater than the other, the forces are unbalanced. This means that the object will move in the direction of the larger force.

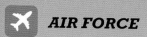 ## AIR FORCE

The thin shape of aeroplanes helps them to be streamlined.

The streamlined shape of aeroplanes helps them to move quickly through the air.

Horizontal wings help to keep the aeroplane steady in the air.

Aeroplanes have a pointed nose to cut through the air.

Unstreamlined aeroplanes would require lots of fuel to push them through the air, which wouldn't be energy- or cost-efficient.

The force created by the cyclist pushing forwards is greater than the air resistance, so the cyclist moves forwards.

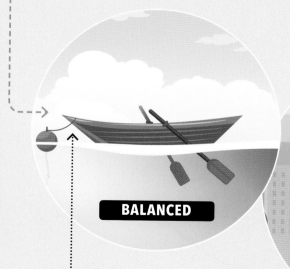

BALANCED

Boats float because the weight of the boat is balanced by the upthrust (pushing force) of the water.

UNBALANCED

MAGNETS

Magnets are objects that have an invisible force that pulls on magnetic materials from a distance. This force is called magnetism.

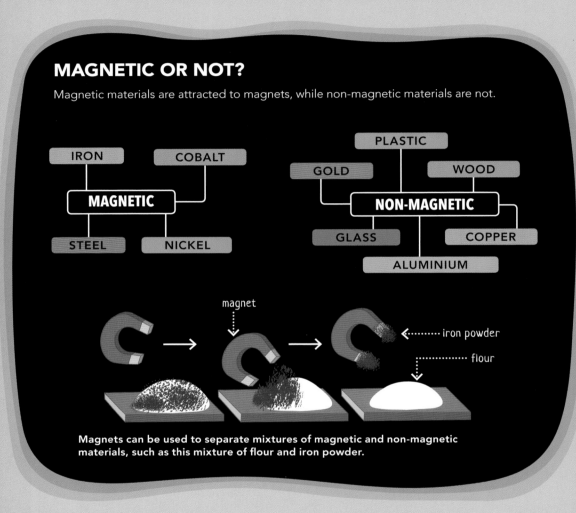

MAGNETIC OR NOT?

Magnetic materials are attracted to magnets, while non-magnetic materials are not.

IRON   COBALT

MAGNETIC

STEEL   NICKEL

PLASTIC   GOLD   WOOD

NON-MAGNETIC

GLASS   COPPER

ALUMINIUM

magnet

iron powder

flour

Magnets can be used to separate mixtures of magnetic and non-magnetic materials, such as this mixture of flour and iron powder.

POLES

The ends of a magnet are called poles. One end is the north pole and the other is the south pole. If you try to join two magnets together at the same pole, the poles will push away from each other or 'repel'. However, if you put two different poles together, they will attract each other and pull together.

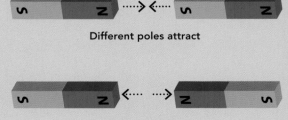

S   N ····> <···· S   N

Different poles attract

S   N <···· ····> N   S

Same poles repel

MAGNETIC FIELDS

A magnet creates a magnetic field around it. This is the area that is affected by its magnetism. Magnetic fields are drawn as lines around a magnet. The closer the lines, the stronger the magnetic force. It is strongest at the poles.

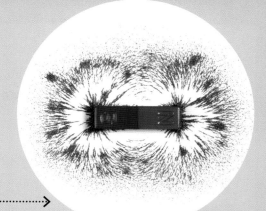

We can see the effects of a magnetic field for ourselves with iron filings and a magnet. The iron filings are attracted to the strongest areas of the magnetic field. ·············>

MAGNETIC EARTH

Earth is a magnet because it has magnetic materials in its core, such as iron and nickel. Like any magnet, it has a north pole and a south pole. Earth's magnetic north and south poles are close to the geographic north and south poles (the most northerly and southerly points). We can use Earth's magnetic field for navigation, because compasses point to the magnetic north pole. Many animals, such as birds, can sense Earth's magnetic field and also use it for navigation.

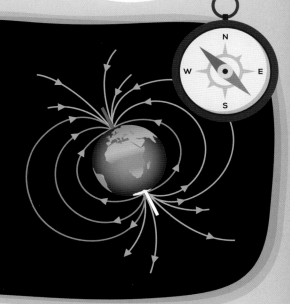

USES FOR MAGNETS

We can use magnets for many amazing things:

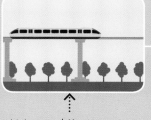

high-speed Maglev trains are held above the tracks by magnets (this reduces friction so that they can move faster)

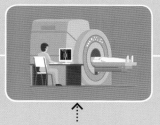

to look inside people's bodies to see if they are hurt or ill in a MRI scan

to store data in computers

to create sound in speakers and headphones

35 Which force pulls objects towards each other?

36 Which objects have more gravity – light objects or heavy objects?

37 What is friction?

38 Why is it easy to ski across smooth ice and snow?

39 How does resistance affect the speed of an object?

40 What does streamlined mean?

41 Which part of an aeroplane helps to keep it steady in the air?

42 Why do boats float on water?

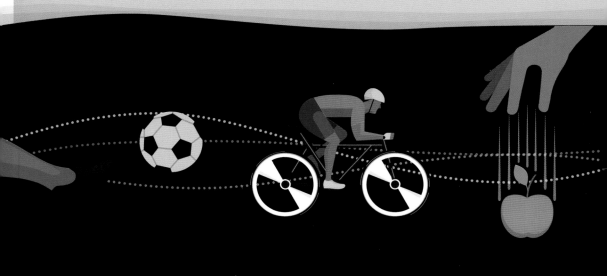

---> **43** What happens to an object when the forces acting on it are unbalanced?

44 Name two magnetic materials.

45 What are the poles of a magnet?

46 What happens if you try to join two magnets together at the same pole?

47 What is a magnetic field?

48 Why is Earth a magnet?

49 Name a type of animal that uses Earth's magnetic field for navigation.

50 How do high-speed Maglev trains use magnets?

51 How are magnets used in computers?

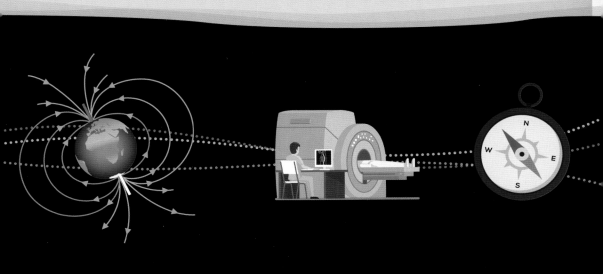

MATERIALS

Materials have different properties, such as being hard, soft, resistant or fragile. A material's properties make it useful for certain purposes.

NATURAL AND HUMAN-MADE MATERIALS

We can divide materials into two categories: natural and human-made. Natural materials are taken straight from nature. Human-made materials are made by people from natural resources.

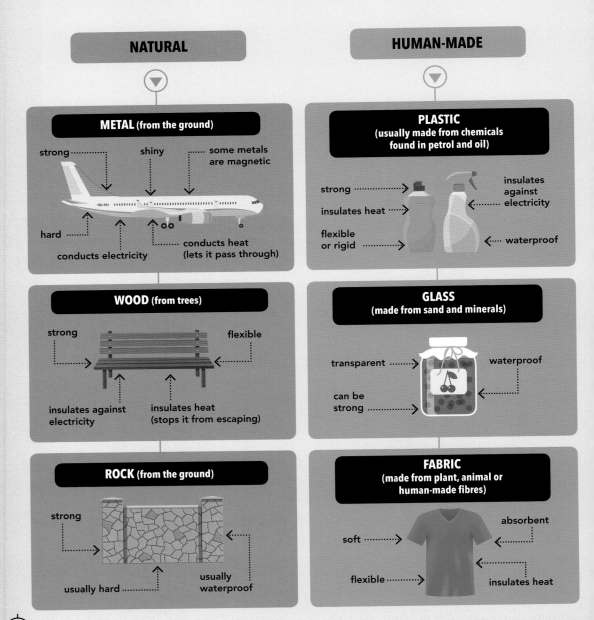

NATURAL

METAL (from the ground)

strong ·········· shiny ·········· some metals are magnetic

hard ········

conducts electricity

conducts heat (lets it pass through)

WOOD (from trees)

strong ········· flexible

insulates against electricity

insulates heat (stops it from escaping)

ROCK (from the ground)

strong ········

usually hard ··········· usually waterproof

HUMAN-MADE

PLASTIC (usually made from chemicals found in petrol and oil)

strong ·············· insulates against electricity

insulates heat ·······

flexible or rigid ··········· waterproof

GLASS (made from sand and minerals)

transparent ········· waterproof

can be strong ·········

FABRIC (made from plant, animal or human-made fibres)

absorbent

soft ········

flexible ·········· insulates heat

LONG-LIFE MATERIALS

Human-made materials, such as plastic, are often durable. They last a long time without breaking down. This can be useful, as we don't want some objects to be fragile or break easily. However, this is a problem when these materials are thrown away, as they will not decompose for hundreds or even thousands of years. They often end up in the ocean or in landfill sites, polluting natural environments.

RECYCLING MATERIALS

Some materials can be reused or recycled. We can reuse the object as it is, or break down the material and reshape it into something else. This is good for the environment, as less of these materials end up in landfill. It also uses fewer natural resources, such as oil for making plastic.

GLASS   PAPER   PLASTIC   METAL

SOLIDS, LIQUIDS AND GASES

Materials can exist in different states. They can be solids, liquids or gases.

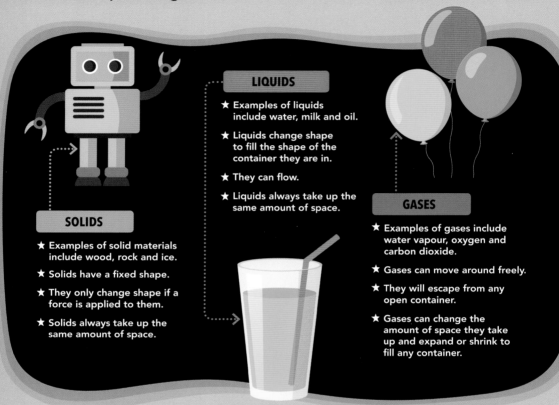

LIQUIDS

★ Examples of liquids include water, milk and oil.

★ Liquids change shape to fill the shape of the container they are in.

★ They can flow.

★ Liquids always take up the same amount of space.

SOLIDS

★ Examples of solid materials include wood, rock and ice.

★ Solids have a fixed shape.

★ They only change shape if a force is applied to them.

★ Solids always take up the same amount of space.

GASES

★ Examples of gases include water vapour, oxygen and carbon dioxide.

★ Gases can move around freely.

★ They will escape from any open container.

★ Gases can change the amount of space they take up and expand or shrink to fill any container.

PARTICLES

Every object is made up of tiny particles. The way in which these particles are arranged determines whether the object is a solid, a liquid or a gas.

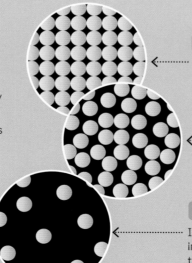

SOLID

In a solid, the particles are fixed together and can't move around.

LIQUID

In a liquid, the particles can move around each other, but they can't move closer together or further apart.

GAS

In a gas, the particles can move freely in any direction and can move closer together or further apart.

CHANGING STATES

Heating or cooling can make a material change state.

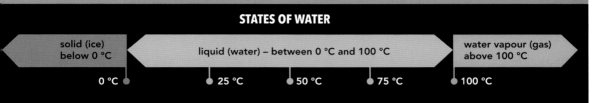

STATES OF WATER

| solid (ice) below 0 °C | liquid (water) – between 0 °C and 100 °C | water vapour (gas) above 100 °C |

0 °C   25 °C   50 °C   75 °C   100 °C

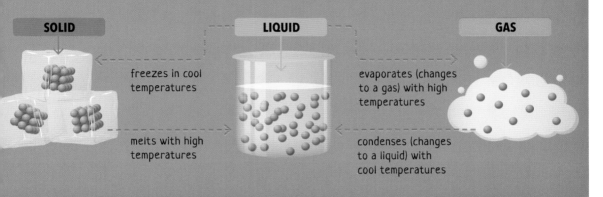

SOLID

LIQUID

GAS

freezes in cool temperatures

evaporates (changes to a gas) with high temperatures

melts with high temperatures

condenses (changes to a liquid) with cool temperatures

BACK AND FORTH

Some changes in state are reversible. If the temperature is changed, the object will return to its original state. For example, if you apply heat to chocolate, it melts and turns from solid to liquid. However, if the liquid chocolate cools down, it turns back into a solid.

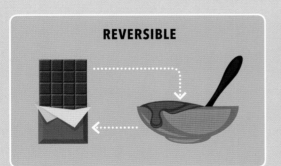

REVERSIBLE

IRREVERSIBLE

Other changes are irreversible. For example, if you bake (heat) liquid cake mix, it forms a solid cake. The solid cake can't be turned back into liquid cake mix by cooling it down.

GO QUIZ YOURSELF!

52 What is a human-made material?

53 Name two properties of metal.

54 What does it mean to conduct heat?

55 What is plastic usually made from?

56 Which material is transparent, waterproof and often strong?

57 What is the environmental problem of plastics and other durable human-made materials?

58 Name one benefit of recycling.

59 Which state of matter has a fixed shape?

----> **60** How do you make a solid change shape?

61 Which state of matter can change the amount of space it takes up?

62 What tiny things are all objects made up of?

63 How do particles in a liquid behave?

64 If heat is applied to a solid, which state does it change into?

65 What is evaporation?

66 At which temperature does water change from liquid to solid?

67 Give an example of a reversible change.

68 What is an irreversible change?

LIVING THINGS

Plants and animals are both living things. They have seven main features in common, but they are different in other ways.

| ANIMALS | ALL LIVING THINGS: | PLANTS |

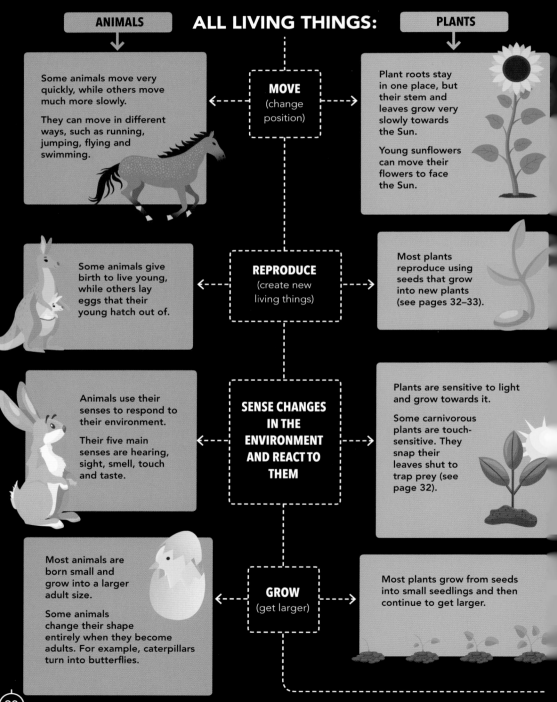

ANIMALS

Some animals move very quickly, while others move much more slowly.

They can move in different ways, such as running, jumping, flying and swimming.

MOVE
(change position)

PLANTS

Plant roots stay in one place, but their stem and leaves grow very slowly towards the Sun.

Young sunflowers can move their flowers to face the Sun.

Some animals give birth to live young, while others lay eggs that their young hatch out of.

REPRODUCE
(create new living things)

Most plants reproduce using seeds that grow into new plants (see pages 32–33).

Animals use their senses to respond to their environment.

Their five main senses are hearing, sight, smell, touch and taste.

SENSE CHANGES IN THE ENVIRONMENT AND REACT TO THEM

Plants are sensitive to light and grow towards it.

Some carnivorous plants are touch-sensitive. They snap their leaves shut to trap prey (see page 32).

Most animals are born small and grow into a larger adult size.

Some animals change their shape entirely when they become adults. For example, caterpillars turn into butterflies.

GROW
(get larger)

Most plants grow from seeds into small seedlings and then continue to get larger.

Animals get nutrients by eating other living things.

Some eat plants (herbivores), while others (carnivores) eat other animals.

Omnivores eat both plants and other animals.

TAKE IN NUTRIENTS

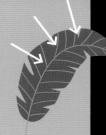

Plants make their own food from sunlight, carbon dioxide and water through a process called photosynthesis.

They also need nutrients, which most plants absorb from the soil.

Animals require oxygen to release energy from food.

Many animals breathe air to get oxygen into their bodies. This oxygen is used to release energy from food. The oxygen reacts with glucose in food to release energy.

Some water animals, such as fish, have gills that absorb oxygen from water.

RESPIRE
(get energy from food)

Plants need oxygen to get energy from the food that they produce.

They absorb oxygen from the air through holes in their leaves.

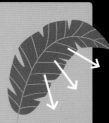

Animals release waste gases, such as carbon dioxide, by breathing out.

Other waste products are excreted in urine.

EXCRETE
(release waste products)

Waste gases and unwanted water are released from plants through tiny holes in their leaves.

OTHER LIVING THINGS

Fungi and bacteria aren't plants or animals – they are their own types of living thing.

Bacteria are very small organisms that only have one cell. Some carry out photosynthesis like plants, while others eat other organisms.

Mushrooms and toadstools are both examples of fungi. They don't produce their own food like plants. They get their nutrients from other plants or animals, often dead ones.

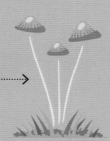

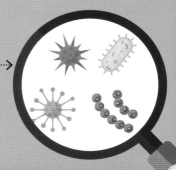

PLANTS

There are many different shapes and sizes of plants on Earth. People depend on plants for food, oxygen and as a key part of all natural habitats.

FLOWERS, FRUIT AND SEEDS

Flowering plants reproduce by producing flowers, fruit and seeds. First, they grow bright, colourful flowers that are pollinated (fertilised) by insects or the wind. The fruit that grows from a pollinated flower contains the seeds. Animals and the wind help to carry the seeds to new areas where they grow into new plants.

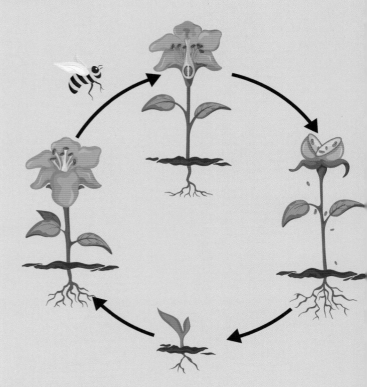

WEIRD AND WONDERFUL PLANTS

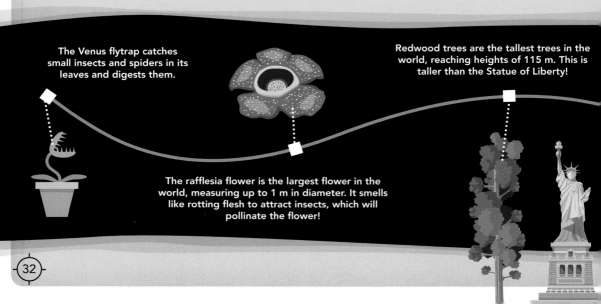

The Venus flytrap catches small insects and spiders in its leaves and digests them.

Redwood trees are the tallest trees in the world, reaching heights of 115 m. This is taller than the Statue of Liberty!

The rafflesia flower is the largest flower in the world, measuring up to 1 m in diameter. It smells like rotting flesh to attract insects, which will pollinate the flower!

HOW PLANTS GROW

Seeds need to be in a warm, wet environment to germinate (start to grow).

① First, the seed case breaks open.

② The roots begin to grow downwards.

③ A shoot starts growing upwards.

⑤ Above ground, the stem and leaves grow out of the shoot.

④ Eventually the shoot breaks through the soil and up towards the light.

TREES THROUGH THE YEAR

Deciduous trees look different throughout the year. The leaves of deciduous trees turn yellow, orange and red in autumn and then fall off in winter. These trees regrow their leaves in spring. Evergreen trees do not change colour. They lose and regrow their leaves gradually throughout the year

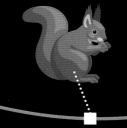

Scientists managed to grow a plant from a 32,000-year-old seed that had been buried by a squirrel and covered in ice!

The coco de mer is the largest seed in the world! This giant seed can measure 50 cm in diameter and weigh up to 25 kg! It comes from a type of palm tree found on the Seychelles islands in the Indian Ocean.

69 How many features do living things have in common?

70 How do plants move?

71 Name two ways that animals reproduce.

72 What are the five main animal senses?

73 What is photosynthesis?

74 How do animals get oxygen for respiration?

75 How do plants release waste gases and unwanted water?

76 Which group of living things does the mushroom belong to?

77 Name something that helps to pollinate flowers.

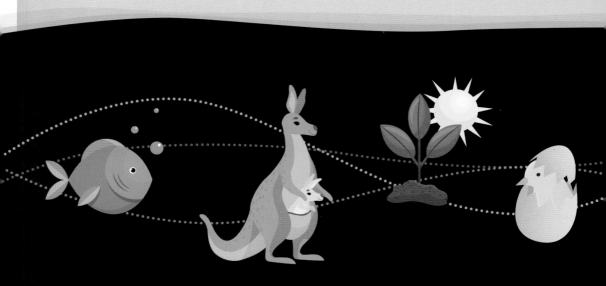

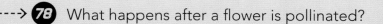 **78** What happens after a flower is pollinated?

79 What kind of environment do seeds need to germinate?

80 What happens to deciduous trees in autumn?

81 What is an evergreen tree?

82 Which plant catches small insects and spiders?

83 What is the largest flower in the world?

84 What are the tallest trees in the world?

85 How much can a coco de mer seed weigh?

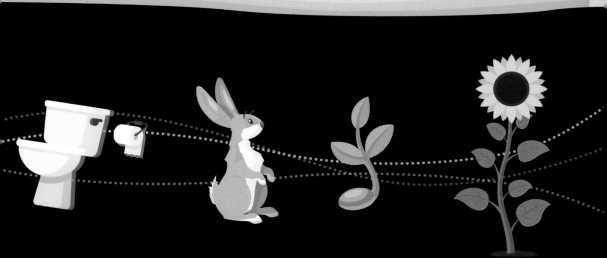

ANCIENT SCIENCE

In the past, ancient civilisations tried to understand the world around them. Some of their theories were spot on, while others we now know were incorrect. They also designed incredible inventions that changed society and helped create the world we live in today.

PREHISTORIC PEOPLE

Several important inventions revolutionised prehistoric times. When people learned how to work with bronze and iron, they were able to replace their stone, wood and bone tools with superior metal ones. This made tasks, such as farming and construction, much easier.

 MAKING BRONZE

Metalworking is an ancient technique. Some metalworking today is still done in this way.

To make bronze, copper and tin are melted together.

The liquid bronze is poured into a mould in the shape of the tool or part that is needed.

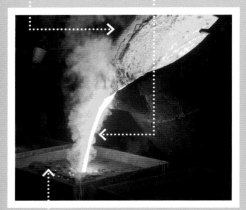

The liquid bronze is left to cool in the mould into a solid.

ANCIENT CHINA

Some of the most important inventions came from ancient China. In the second century CE, paper was invented in China. From there, it spread slowly across the planet, changing society forever. The ancient Chinese also invented gunpowder, which they used in weapons. They also used gunpowder to make the world's first fireworks!

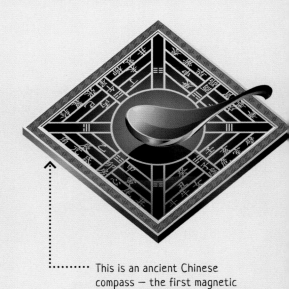

This is an ancient Chinese compass – the first magnetic compass to be invented. The spoon in the centre was made of a magnetic material.

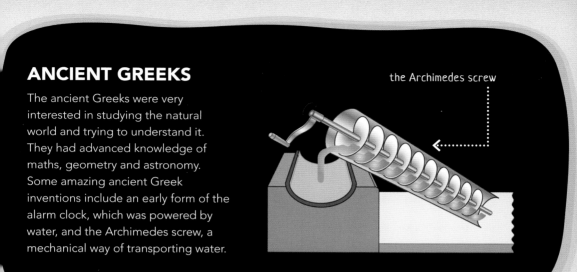

ANCIENT GREEKS

the Archimedes screw

The ancient Greeks were very interested in studying the natural world and trying to understand it. They had advanced knowledge of maths, geometry and astronomy. Some amazing ancient Greek inventions include an early form of the alarm clock, which was powered by water, and the Archimedes screw, a mechanical way of transporting water.

ISLAMIC SCIENTISTS

Scientists in the early Islamic civilisation translated many ancient scientific texts from the ancient Greeks and the Romans. They studied these ancient ideas and then developed them further, based on their own research!

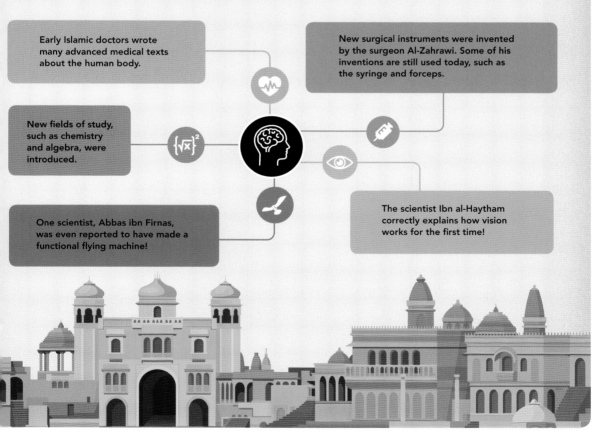

Early Islamic doctors wrote many advanced medical texts about the human body.

New surgical instruments were invented by the surgeon Al-Zahrawi. Some of his inventions are still used today, such as the syringe and forceps.

New fields of study, such as chemistry and algebra, were introduced.

The scientist Ibn al-Haytham correctly explains how vision works for the first time!

One scientist, Abbas ibn Firnas, was even reported to have made a functional flying machine!

AMAZING INVENTIONS

Scientists and engineers have created incredible machines that help to make everyday life easier and improve our understanding of science.

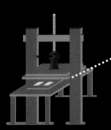

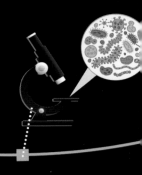

1450

Johannes Gutenberg designs the printing press. Before the printing press, everything was written by hand, which was very slow. Printed materials, such as scientific research and theories, could be created and shared much more quickly and easily with a wider range of people across different countries.

1590

The first compound microscope is created by Dutch glasses makers – Hans and Zacharias Janssen. Scientists were able to see objects in close detail and saw a whole new miniature world for the first time.

1843

Ada Lovelace designs the first computer program, based on Babbage's Analytical Engine.

1834

Charles Babbage creates the Analytical Engine – a type of mechanical computer.

1864

The first bicycle with pedals is created. Before this, people had to push bicycles forwards with their legs! Adding pedals allowed cyclists to travel faster and use less energy.

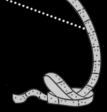

1903

The Wright brothers take the first aeroplane flight. This form of transport became safer and more popular over time and is now used to transport millions of people around the world every day.

1876

Alexander Graham Bell demonstrates his new invention – the telephone. The telephone revolutionised communication, allowing people to quickly contact each other across great distances.

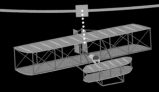

1658

Christiaan Huygens creates the pendulum clock. The invention helped people to keep track of time in a more accurate way.

1609

Galileo Galilei begins to observe space using a telescope. He saw faraway objects, such as the surface of the Moon, in detail for the first time.

1783

The Montgolfier brothers take the first public flight in a hot air balloon. This was the first step towards human flight and a chance to see the world from a whole new angle.

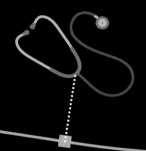

1800

Alessandro Volta invents the first electric battery – the voltaic pile. Scientists finally had a reliable source of electricity for their experiments.

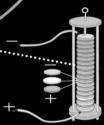

1816

René Laënnec invents the stethoscope. Doctors could finally use sounds from inside the body to help diagnose their patients.

1989

Tim Berners-Lee creates the World Wide Web. This allowed people to access the Internet and connect with each other.

1920s

John Logie Baird demonstrates TV for the first time. This invention has brought information and entertainment to people in their homes.

1973

The first mobile phone call is made. The first mobile phones were large and expensive, but over time, they have become smaller and more affordable.

86 How did metalworking make life easier for prehistoric people?

87 Which two metals are melted together to make bronze?

88 When was paper invented?

89 Name two uses for gunpowder in ancient China.

90 Which civilisation invented the first magnetic compass?

91 What powered the alarm clock designed by the ancient Greeks?

92 What was the Archimedes screw?

93 Name a surgical instrument invented by the early Islamic surgeon Al-Zahrawi.

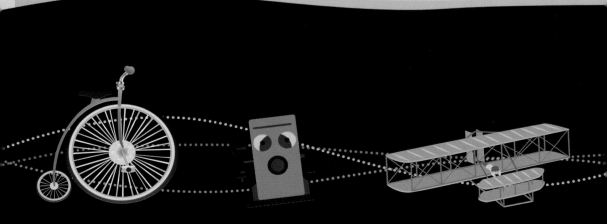

94 What did Galileo Galilei observe with his telescope?

95 What was the voltaic pile?

96 Which vehicle did the Montgolfier brothers fly for the first time in 1783?

97 Who designed the first computer program?

98 How did adding pedals to bicycles help cyclists?

99 What did Alexander Graham Bell invent?

100 In which decade did John Logie Baird demonstrate TV for the first time?

101 When was the first mobile phone call made?

102 Who created the World Wide Web?

$\{\sqrt{x}\}^2$

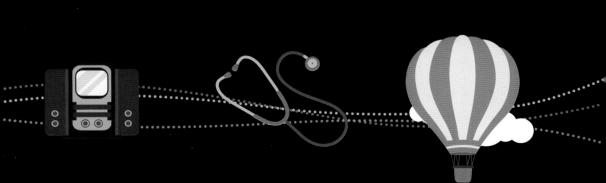

THE FUTURE OF SCIENCE

The scientists of today are working hard on the breakthroughs and inventions of the future. In our lifetime, we will probably see many incredible discoveries that will make life easier and help us to understand science better.

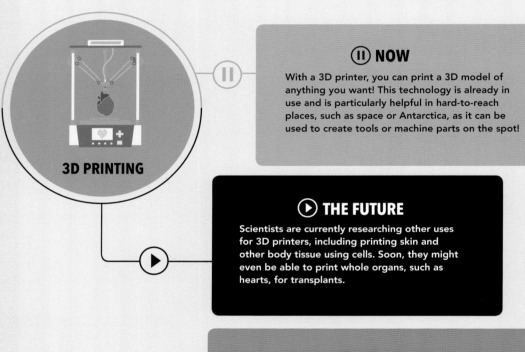

3D PRINTING

⏸ NOW

With a 3D printer, you can print a 3D model of anything you want! This technology is already in use and is particularly helpful in hard-to-reach places, such as space or Antarctica, as it can be used to create tools or machine parts on the spot!

▶ THE FUTURE

Scientists are currently researching other uses for 3D printers, including printing skin and other body tissue using cells. Soon, they might even be able to print whole organs, such as hearts, for transplants.

⏸ NOW

We are becoming more and more conscious of our negative impact on the planet. Scientists are working hard to find ways to reduce the damage that we do. Some current solutions are creating fuels from waste, designing biodegradable alternatives to plastic and making artificial meat rather than raising animals on farms.

SUSTAINABLE SOLUTIONS

▶ THE FUTURE

Scientists will continue to come up with solutions to help the environment. These could be new, cleaner fuels or ways of removing plastic from the ocean. A major focus is to find ways of reducing the greenhouse effect, and therefore global warming, by removing excess carbon dioxide from the atmosphere.

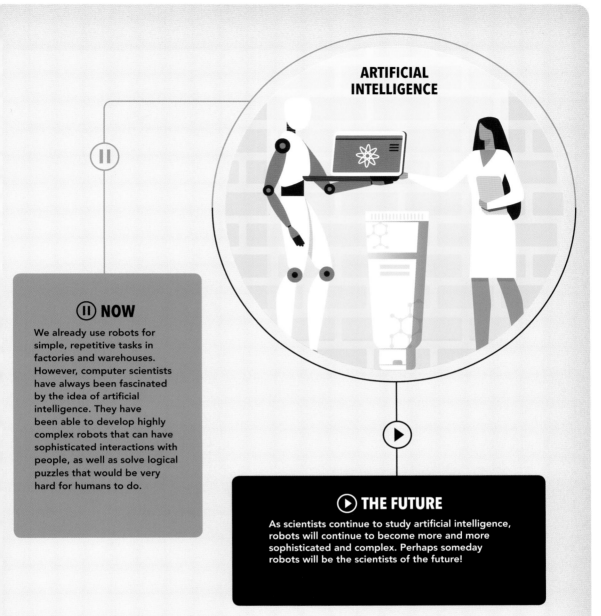

ARTIFICIAL INTELLIGENCE

⏸ NOW

We already use robots for simple, repetitive tasks in factories and warehouses. However, computer scientists have always been fascinated by the idea of artificial intelligence. They have been able to develop highly complex robots that can have sophisticated interactions with people, as well as solve logical puzzles that would be very hard for humans to do.

▶ THE FUTURE

As scientists continue to study artificial intelligence, robots will continue to become more and more sophisticated and complex. Perhaps someday robots will be the scientists of the future!

QUIZ TIME!

After you've finished testing yourself, why not use this book to make a quiz to test your friends and family? You could take questions from each section to make different rounds, or mix and match across the book for a general knowledge science quiz. You can even make up your own quiz questions! Use these future of science facts to get you started. For example, 'How is 3D printing used in space?' or 'What kind of tasks are robots used for?'

ANSWERS

1   The science of life and living things, or plants, animals and the human body

2   Physics

3   Because gravity pulls on the pancake batter evenly, forming it into a circle

4   The scorpion

5   An object that gives off light

6   Vampire squid, fireflies, anglerfish, crystal jellyfish, some millipedes (and scorpions)

7   Opaque

8   When a translucent or opaque object blocks light

9   Black

10   Because sunlight reflects off tiny particles in the air and scatters mostly blue light across the sky

11   Low-pitched

12   Dogs

13   Decibels

14   60 decibels

15   The eruption of the Krakatoa volcano in 1883

16   Because the walls of a tunnel are hard and reflect sounds, creating echoes

17   A system in which ships use echoes to find objects underwater

18   Light, sound, heat, movement, electrical and chemical

19   Chemical energy

20   Electrical energy is converted into heat energy

21   Movement energy and heat energy

22   Moving water spins a turbine, which powers a generator that generates electricity

23   A gas that gathers in the atmosphere and traps heat from the Sun near to Earth's surface

24   Asthma, certain types of cancer

25   0.8 °C

26   Current and static

27   Light bulb, motor, buzzer, battery, wire or switch

28   Electricity does not flow around the circuit

29   Plastic, wood, glass, rubber

30   Static electricity

31   7.74 seconds

32   Lightning

33   To send messages to and from the brain or to make the heart beat

34   The electric eel

35   Gravity

36   Heavy objects

37   The force that acts on an object when it moves against another object

38   Because there is very little friction

39   It slows the object down

40   With a smooth shape

41   Horizontal wings

42   Because the weight of the boat pushing down is balanced by the upthrust (pushing force) of the water pushing up

43   It will move in the direction of the larger force

44   Iron, steel, nickel or cobalt

45   The two ends of a magnet

46   They will repel

47   The area around a magnet affected by its magnetism

48   Because it has magnetic materials, such as iron and nickel, in its core

49   A bird

50   The magnets hold the train above the tracks, which reduces friction so that the train can move faster

51   To store data

52   A material made by people using natural resources

53   Strong, hard, shiny, conducts electricity, conducts heat, often magnetic

54 Let heat pass through

55 Chemicals found in petrol and oil

56 Glass

57 They won't decompose for hundreds or even thousands of years, so they pollute natural areas

58 Fewer objects end up in landfill and fewer resources are used to create new materials

59 Solid

60 By applying a force to it

61 Gas

62 Particles

63 In a liquid, the particles can move around each other, but they can't move closer together or further apart

64 Liquid

65 When heat is applied to a liquid and it changes into a gas

66 0 °C

67 Chocolate melting from solid to liquid

68 When something changes state, but can't return to its original state

69 Seven

70 Their stem and leaves grow slowly towards the Sun

71 Give birth to live young or lay eggs that young hatch out of

72 Hearing, sight, smell, touch and taste

73 The process in which plants use sunlight, carbon dioxide and water to produce their own food

74 They breathe in air, which contains oxygen, or absorb oxygen from water using gills

75 Through tiny holes in their leaves

76 Fungi

77 Insects or the wind

78 It grows into a fruit, which contains seeds

79 Warm and wet

80 Their leaves turn yellow, orange and red

81 A tree that loses and regrows its leaves gradually throughout the year

82 The Venus flytrap

83 The rafflesia flower

84 Redwood trees

85 Up to 25 kg

86 Metal tools made farming and construction easier

87 Copper and tin

88 The second century CE

89 Weapons and fireworks

90 The ancient Chinese

91 Water

92 A mechanical way of transporting water

93 The syringe or forceps

94 Objects in space, such as the surface of the Moon

95 The first electric battery

96 The hot air balloon

97 Ada Lovelace

98 They could go faster and use less energy

99 The telephone

100 The 1920s

101 1973

102 Tim Berners–Lee

HOW WELL DID YOU DO?

100–102 ---> QUIZMASTER

75–99 -----> QUIZTASTIC

50–74 ------> QUIZ ON

25–49 -------> QUIZLING

0–24 --------> QUIZ IT AGAIN

GLOSSARY

amplitude – the height of a wave

artificial intelligence – developing computers and robots that have intelligence similar to that of a human

atom – the smallest unit that an element can be divided into

biodegradable – something that breaks down naturally without hurting the environment

circuit – an electrical system made up of an electrical source and wires

component – an element in a circuit, such as a light bulb or motor

conductor – a material that electricity or heat can pass through

element – a substance that can't be broken down into other substances

friction – a force that acts on an object moving across a surface

global warming – the increase in temperature on Earth

gravity – a force that pulls things towards each other

greenhouse gas – a gas that gathers in Earth's atmosphere, trapping light from the Sun close to Earth's surface

insulator – a material that electricity or heat can't pass through

magnetic field – the area affected by a magnet's magnetism

navigation – finding the right direction to travel in

particle – a very small piece of something

photosynthesis – the process by which plants make energy

pitch – how high or low a sound is

pole – one end of a magnet

reproduce – to produce young animals or new plants

resistance – friction that works on objects moving through air or water

respire – to get energy from food

state of matter – whether something is a solid, a liquid or a gas

streamlined – designed in a way that makes it easier to move through air or water

turbine – a type of machine in which liquids or gases power a wheel that generates electricity

vibrate – to shake quickly

volume – how loud or quiet a sound is

FURTHER INFORMATION

BOOKS

Extreme Science series
by Jon Richards (Wayland, 2019)

Science in a Flash series
by Georgia Amson-Bradshaw (Franklin Watts, 2018)

Science in Infographics series
by Jon Richards and Ed Simkins (Wayland, 2017)

WEBSITES

www.britannica.com/story/history-of-technology-timeline
Explore a timeline of some of the greatest inventions of all time.

www.coolkidfacts.com/electricity-facts/
Discover some 'shocking' facts about electricity!

www.bbc.co.uk/bitesize/articles/zsgwwxs
Learn more about the states of matter – solids, liquids and gases.

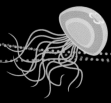
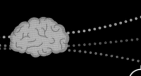

INDEX

3D printing 42

ancient China 36
ancient Greece 37
animals 4, 5, 6, 8, 15, 21, 30–31, 32, 42
artificial intelligence 43

biology 4

chemistry 4, 37
circuits 14

early Islamic civilisation 37
electricity 5, 6, 12, 13, 14–15, 24, 39
energy 4, 12–13, 14, 31

flowers 30, 32
forces 4, 5, 18–19, 20, 21, 26
friction 18, 19, 21
fruit 32

gases 5, 13, 26, 27, 31
global warming 13
gravity 5, 18

inventions 36, 37, 38–39

light 5, 6–7, 12, 30, 31, 33
lightning 15
liquids 4, 5, 26, 27, 36
living things 4, 30–31

magnets 4, 20–21, 24, 36
materials 6, 7, 14, 15, 20, 24–25, 26, 27, 36

particles 5, 7, 15, 26
physics 4
plants 4, 5, 12, 24, 30, 31, 32–33
prehistory 36

recycling 25
resistance 19

shadows 7
solids 5, 26, 27, 36
sound 5, 8–9, 12, 21
sustainable science 42

water 5, 7, 9, 13, 14, 19, 24, 26, 27, 31, 37
waves 4, 5, 8, 9

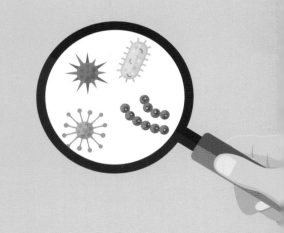